PIANO/VOCAL
ELLA FITZGERALD
ORIGINAL KEYS FOR SINGERS

Transcribed by Forrest Mankowski

Cover Photo: The Frank Driggs Collection

ISBN 0-634-06342-1

7777 W. BLUEMOUND RD. P.O. BOX 13819 MILWAUKEE, WI 53213

For all works contained herein:
Unauthorized copying, arranging, adapting, recording or public performance is an infringement of copyright.
Infringers are liable under the law.

Visit Hal Leonard Online at
www.halleonard.com

ELLA FITZGERALD

4	BIOGRAPHY
150	DISCOGRAPHY
6	A-Tisket, A-Tasket
14	Black Coffee
19	But Not For Me
24	Cheek To Cheek
31	Easy To Love (You'd Be So Easy To Love)
36	Embraceable You
41	Ev'ry Time We Say Goodbye
44	How Long Has This Been Going On?
47	I Got It Bad And That Ain't Good
54	I'm Beginning To See The Light
62	I'm Putting All My Eggs In One Basket
70	I've Got My Love To Keep Me Warm
75	If You Can't Sing It (You'll Have To Swing It)
82	Ill Wind (You're Blowin' Me No Good)
86	It Don't Mean A Thing (If It Ain't Got That Swing)
100	Just One Of Those Things
93	The Lady Is A Tramp
108	Let's Call The Whole Thing Off
116	Lullaby Of Birdland
121	Midnight Sun
128	Misty
132	Oh, Lady Be Good!
137	Satin Doll
140	Stompin' At The Savoy
143	Take The "A" Train

ELLA FITZGERALD

The music of Ella Fitzgerald will be forever remembered through her sultry ballads, her prodigious scatting, and her immortal renditions of American standards. With the voice of an angel, she seduced the world for half a century. During her lifetime, she was not only appreciated by her fans, but was revered among her fellow jazz musicians as an equal, a jazz giant, and an innovator.

Ella was born on April 25, 1917 in Newport News, Virginia. Moving to New York City with her mother, Tempie, when she was just a babe in arms, she began her education at Public School 10 in the city of Yonkers in September 1923. Despite her situation as an impoverished girl north of Harlem, she was a continually cheerful and outgoing girl determined to make it in show business — as a dancer.

Although a fine dancer, she was thankfully discovered as a singer at the age of seventeen. In the winter of 1934, Ella sang in and won the Apollo Theatre's Amateur Night contest, as she had drawn the short straw among a group of friends. It was at that performance where she was discovered and brought forward into stardom.

After losing her mother, Ella was an orphan teenager without direction for her musical talent. It was a popular bandleader of the time, Chick Webb, who acted as a surrogate father and mentor during her early career. After joining his band in 1934, it was not very long before she drew large audiences to her performances at Harlem's famous Savoy Ballroom.

In 1938, Ella Fitzgerald recorded "A-Tisket, A-Tasket," a swing rendition of a popular nursery rhyme, arranged by Chick and her. This became a worldwide hit, and today still remains a Swing Era anthem. After Webb's untimely death in 1939, the band was left in Ella's hands. She gave it up after only a few more years, as she was not suited to the demanding whirlwind of running a big band.

The 1940s marked the true beginning of her solo career. She made a series of landmark recordings for Milt Gabler, her producer at Decca, as well as some for Norman Granz, her next producer on the Verve label. In the late 1940s, Ella began to blossom into a bebop singer as well, playing with Dizzy Gillespie's big band for several years. It was during this period that she married jazz bassist Ray Brown, with whom she adopted a child, Ray Brown Jr.

Her career as the world renowned singer finally emerged in 1949, as Granz presented her in the Jazz at the Philharmonic concert series. This popular series featured the finest instrumentalists in jazz, from Charlie Parker to Lester Young. From 1956 to 1964, she recorded some of her most memorable versions of standard songbooks, including those by Cole Porter, Duke Ellington, the Gershwins, Johnny Mercer, Irving Berlin, and Rodgers and Hart.

Ella continued to record and tour through the 1990s, when failing health finally ended her amazing career. On June 15, 1996, Ella Fitzgerald passed on, leaving us a lifetime full of memories through her timeless recordings. Throughout her lifetime, she received accolades from U.S. presidents, universities, the Grammy® awards, and every other person who heard the purity and genius of her music.

She was a singer who responded to the musical imperatives of a song while illuminating the wit within the lyrics. She could spin a melody in any direction, transcending each note and word as sweetly and soulfully as the trumpet of Louie Armstrong, the saxophone of Johnny Hodges, and the clarinet of Benny Goodman. Her love for music was unending, while her passion was unmistakable in every concert she ever performed and every recording she ever made. Every generation that has heard her voice will never forget that there is only one Ella.

A-TISKET, A-TASKET

Words and Music by ELLA FITZGERALD
and VAN ALEXANDER

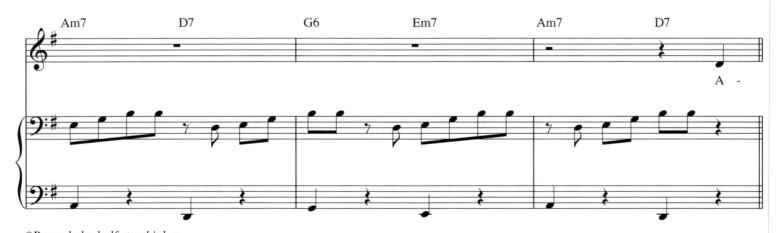

*Recorded a half step higher.

© 1938 (Renewed 1966) EMI Robbins Catalog Inc.
All Rights Controlled by EMI ROBBINS CATALOG INC. (Publishing) and WARNER BROS. PUBLICATIONS U.S. INC. (Print)
All Rights Reserved   Used by Permission

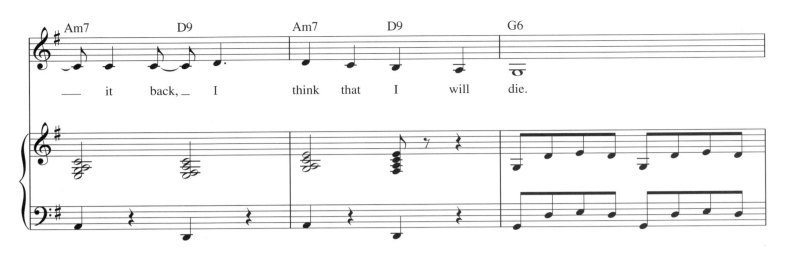
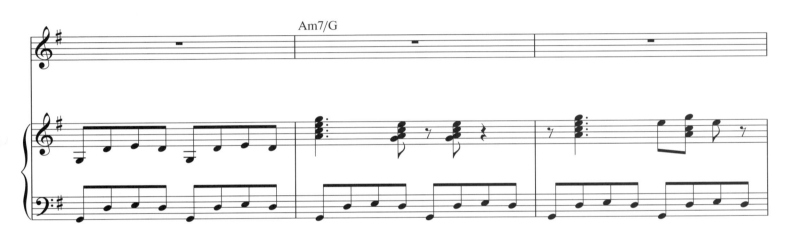

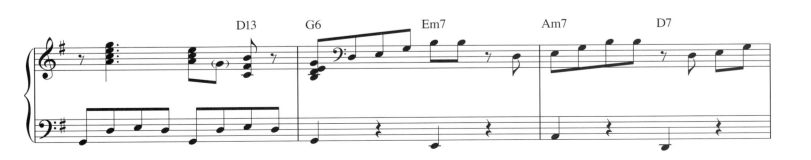

BLACK COFFEE

Words and Music by PAUL FRANCIS WEBSTER
and SONNY BURKE

Copyright © 1948 (Renewed) Webster Music Co. and Sondot Music Corporation
International Copyright Secured   All Rights Reserved

BUT NOT FOR ME

Music and Lyrics by GEORGE GERSHWIN
and IRA GERSHWIN

© 1930 WB MUSIC CORP. (Renewed)
All Rights Reserved   Used by Permission

EASY TO LOVE
(You'd Be So Easy to Love)

Words and Music by
COLE PORTER

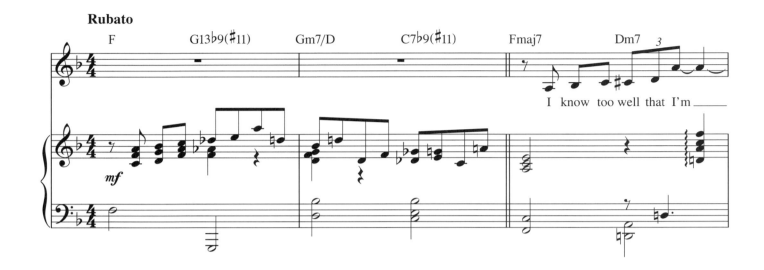

Copyright © 1936 by Chappell & Co.
Copyright Renewed, Assigned to John F. Wharton, Trustee of the Cole Porter Musical and Literary Property Trusts
Chappell & Co. owner of publication and allied rights throughout the world
International Copyright Secured   All Rights Reserved

EMBRACEABLE YOU

Music and Lyrics by GEORGE GERSHWIN
and IRA GERSHWIN

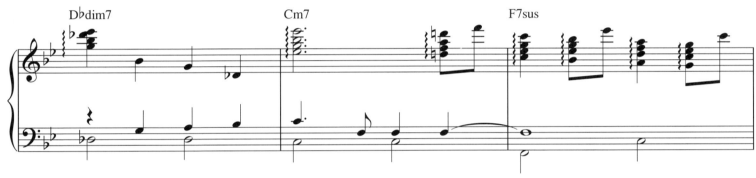

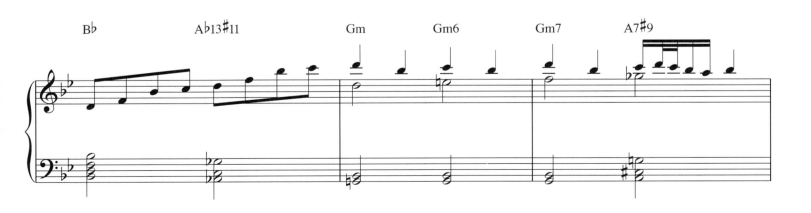

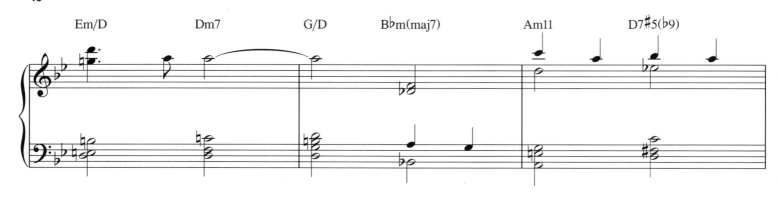

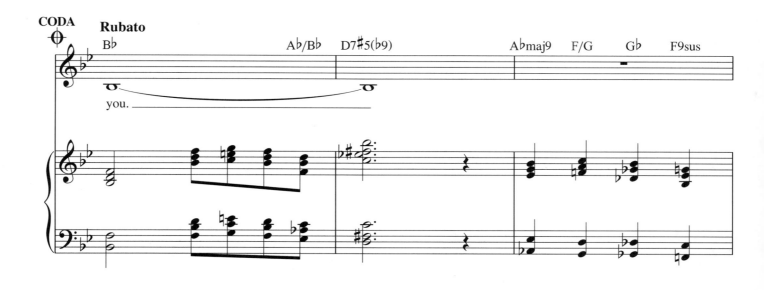
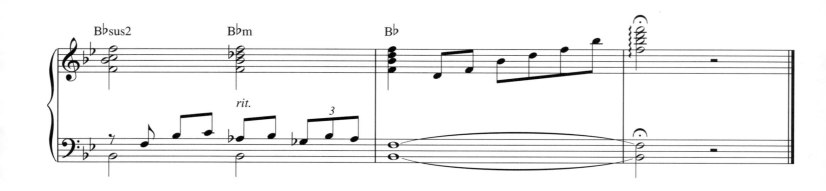

HOW LONG HAS THIS BEEN GOING ON?

Music and Lyrics by GEORGE GERSHWIN
and IRA GERSHWIN

© 1927 WB MUSIC CORP. (Renewed)
All Rights Reserved   Used by Permission

I GOT IT BAD AND THAT AIN'T GOOD

Words by PAUL FRANCIS WEBSTER
Music by DUKE ELLINGTON

I'M BEGINNING TO SEE THE LIGHT

Words and Music by DON GEORGE, JOHNNY HODGES,
DUKE ELLINGTON and HARRY JAMES

I'VE GOT MY LOVE TO KEEP ME WARM
from the 20th Century Fox Motion Picture ON THE AVENUE

Words and Music by
IRVING BERLIN

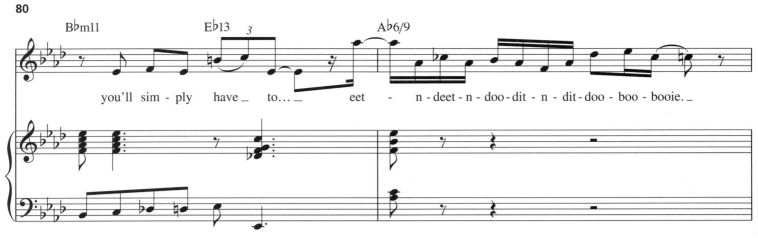
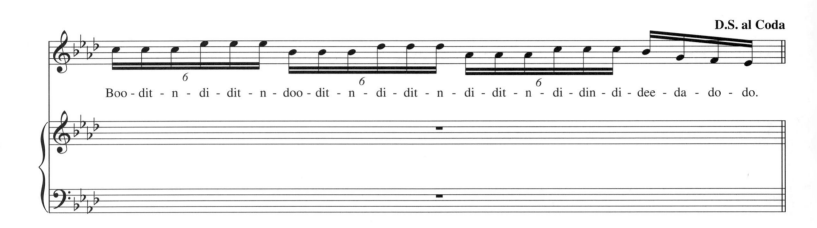
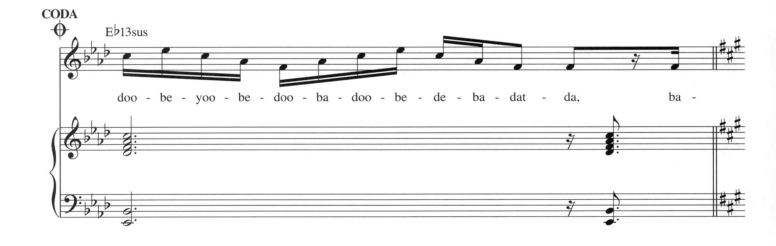
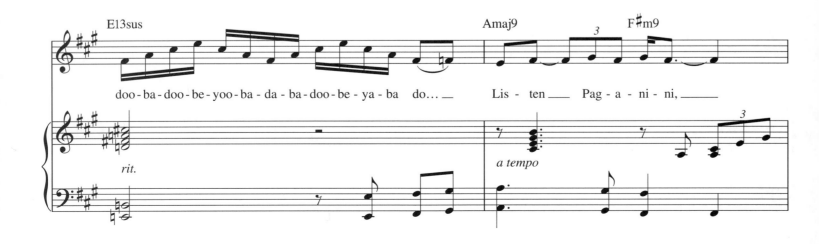

THE LADY IS A TRAMP

Words by LORENZ HART
Music by RICHARD RODGERS

94

JUST ONE OF THOSE THINGS

Words and Music by
COLE PORTER

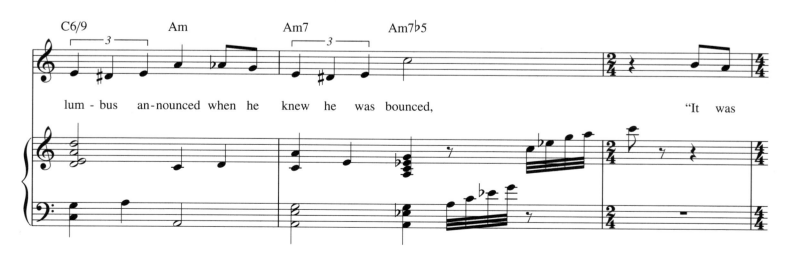

© 1935 WARNER BROS. INC. (Renewed)
All Rights Reserved Used by Permission

LET'S CALL THE WHOLE THING OFF

Music and Lyrics by GEORGE GERSHWIN
and IRA GERSHWIN

© 1936, 1937 (Renewed 1963, 1964) GEORGE GERSHWIN MUSIC and IRA GERSHWIN MUSIC
All Rights Administered by WB MUSIC CORP.
All Rights Reserved   Used by Permission

LULLABY OF BIRDLAND

Words by GEORGE DAVID WEISS
Music by GEORGE SHEARING

Oh, Lull - a - by of Bird - land, that's what I
Have you ev - er heard two tur - tle doves

al - ways hear ___ when you sigh. ___ Nev - er in my word - land
bale and coo ___ when they love? ___ That's the kind of mag - ic

© 1952, 1954 (Renewed 1980, 1982) EMI LONGITUDE MUSIC
All Rights Reserved   International Copyright Secured   Used by Permission

SATIN DOLL

By DUKE ELLINGTON

Copyright © 1953 (Renewed 1981) and Assigned to Famous Music Corporation in the U.S.A.
Rights for the world outside the U.S.A. Controlled by Tempo Music, Inc. c/o Music Sales Corporation
International Copyright Secured   All Rights Reserved

STOMPIN' AT THE SAVOY

Words and Music by BENNY GOODMAN,
EDGAR SAMPSON, CHICK WEBB and ANDY RAZAF

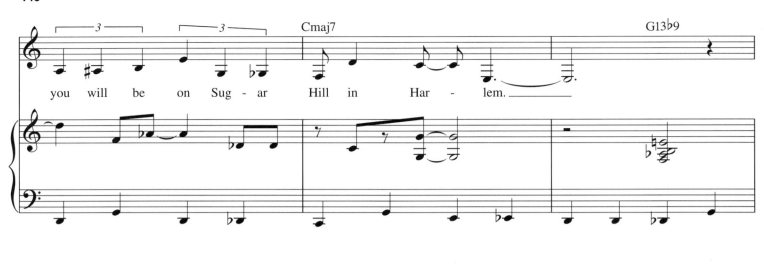

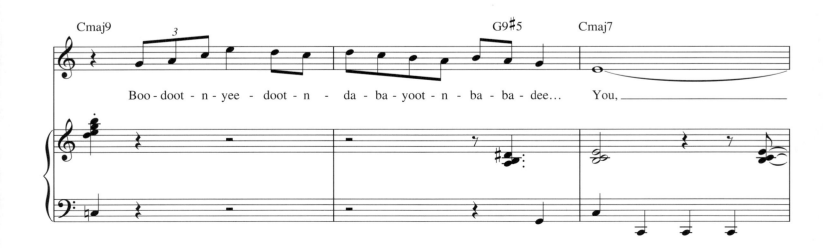

DISCOGRAPHY

A-Tisket, A-Tasket – *Ken Burns JAZZ Collection - Ella Fitzgerald* (Verve 549087-2)

Black Coffee – *The Intimate Ella* (Verve 839838-2)

But Not For Me – *Oh, Lady Be Good!* (ASV 5442)

Cheek To Cheek – *The Irving Berlin Songbook Vol. 1* (Verve 829534-2)

Easy To Love (You'd Be So Easy To Love) – *The Cole Porter Songbook Vol. 1* (Verve 821989-2)

Embraceable You – *Sings The Gershwin Songbook* (Verve 539759-2)

Ev'ry Time We Say Goodbye – *The Cole Porter Songbook Vol. 1* (Verve 821989-2)

How Long Has This Been Going On? – *Oh, Lady Be Good!* (ASV 5442)

I Got It Bad And That Ain't Good – *Sings the Duke Ellington Songbook* (Verve 559248-2)

I'm Beginning To See The Light – *Sings the Duke Ellington Songbook* (Verve 559248-2)

I'm Putting All My Eggs In One Basket – *The Irving Berlin Songbook Vol. 2* (Verve 829535-2)

I've Got My Love To Keep Me Warm – *The Irving Berlin Songbook Vol. 2* (Verve 829535-2)

If You Can't Sing It (You'll Have To Swing It) – *Ella Returns to Berlin* (Verve 837758-2)

Ill Wind (You're Blowin' Me No Good) – *The Best of the Songbooks: The Ballads* (Verve 521867-2)

It Don't Mean A Thing (If It Ain't Got That Swing) – *Sings the Duke Ellington Songbook* (Verve 559248-2)

Just One Of Those Things – *The Cole Porter Songbook Vol. 1* (Verve 821989-2)

The Lady Is A Tramp – *Best of the Songbooks* (Verve 519804-2)

Let's Call The Whole Thing Off – *The Gershwin Songbook* (Verve 539759-2)

Lullaby Of Birdland – *Ken Burns JAZZ Collection – Ella Fitzgerald* (Verve 549087-2)

Midnight Sun – *Best of the Songbooks* (Verve 519804-2)

Misty – *Ella Returns to Berlin* (Verve 837758-2)

Oh, Lady Be Good! - *The Gershwin Songbook* (Verve 539759-2)

Satin Doll – *Sings the Duke Ellington Songbook* (Verve 559248-2)

Stompin' At The Savoy – *Best of Ella Fitzgerald & Louis Armstrong* (Verve 537909-2)

Take The "A" Train – *Sings the Duke Ellington Songbook* (Verve 559248-2)

MORE VOCAL COLLECTIONS
STANDARDS
FROM HAL•LEONARD®

JAZZ VOCAL STANDARDS
Transcriptions of Landmark Arrangements
This outstanding collection assembles and transcribes for piano and voice 18 of the finest recordings in the world of singing. Featured are such legends as: Louis Armstrong ("Ain't Misbehavin'"), Ray Charles ("Georgia on My Mind"), Nat "King" Cole ("Route 66"), Blossom Dearie ("Peel Me a Grape"), Ella Fitzgerald ("Midnight Sun"), Billie Holiday ("Crazy He Calls Me"), Shirley Horn ("Wild Is the Wind"), Frank Sinatra ("I've Got You Under My Skin"), Sarah Vaughan ("An Occasional Man"), and many more. Includes a discography, and notes on each selection.
00310663 Piano/Vocal $19.95

STANDARD BALLADS
These books feature fantastic American standards in new arrangements designed to flatter any singer, with interesting harmonies and accompaniments. The arrangements are in the spirit of the performance tradition of great standards established by singers such as Tony Bennett, Rosemary Clooney, Frank Sinatra, Nat King Cole and Peggy Lee. Keys have been carefully chosen and will be comfortable for most voices. The books contain arrangements for voice and piano accompaniments, and a section of "fake book"-style editions of the arrangements convenient for performing. The companion CD includes wonderful performances of each song by a singer backed by piano, bass and drums, as well as trio accompaniment tracks only for practice or performance.
Songs: All the Things You Are • Autumn Leaves • Call Me Irresponsible • East of the Sun (And West of the Moon) • I Left My Heart in San Francisco • I'll Be Seeing You • In a Sentimental Mood • Isn't It Romantic • The Very Thought of You • The Way You Look Tonight.
00740088 Women's Edition $19.95
00740089 Men's Edition $19.95

TORCH SONGS – WOMEN'S EDITION
The Singer's Series
Fantastic heart-on-the-sleeve American standards in new arrangements designed to flatter any singer, with interesting harmonies and accompaniments. The arrangements are in the spirit of the performance tradition established by singers such as Judy Garland, Tony Bennett, Frank Sinatra, Nat King Cole, Peggy Lee and others. Keys have been carefully chosen and will be comfortable for most voices. The book contains arrangements for voice and piano accompaniment, plus a section of "fake book"-style arrangements convenient for performing. The accompanying CD includes great performances of each song by a singer backed by piano, bass and drums, as well as trio accompaniment tracks only for practice or performance.
00740086 Book/CD Pack $19.95

TORCH SONGS – MEN'S EDITION
The Singer's Series
Great singer/trio arrangements in comfortable singing keys. The Women's Edition includes: Bewitched • Cry Me a River • I Can't Get Started with You • The Man That Got Away • Misty • More Than You Know • My Foolish Heart • My Man (Mon Homme) • Stormy Weather (Keeps Rainin' All the Time) • When the Sun Comes Out. Men's Edition includes: Angel Eyes • Bewitched • Blame It on My Youth • Here's That Rainy Day • I Can't Get Started with You • In the Wee Small Hours of the Morning • Memories of You • Misty • More Than You Know • One for My Baby (And One More for the Road).
00740087 Book/CD Pack $19.95

FOR MORE INFORMATION, SEE YOUR LOCAL MUSIC DEALER, OR WRITE TO:

HAL•LEONARD® CORPORATION
7777 W. BLUEMOUND RD. P.O. BOX 13819 MILWAUKEE, WI 53213

Visit Hal Leonard online at **www.halleonard.com**
Prices, contents & availability subject to change without notice.